The Vision of Wisdom

Holy Inspired by God
Volume II

Gerald Filyaw

The Vision of Wisdom: Holy Inspired by God Volume II
Gerald Filyaw

Scripture quotations marked KJV are from the KING JAMES VERSION of the Bible.

Scripture quotations marked (NLT) are taken from the Holy Bible, New Living Translation, copyright © 1996, 2004, 2007 by Tyndale House Foundation. Used by permission of Tyndale House Publishers, Inc., Carol Stream, Illinois 60188. All rights reserved.

Published by ⬥DiVINE CO.

www.divinepurposepublishing.com
info@divinepurposepublishing.com

ISBN-13: 978-0692609637
ISBN-10: 0692609636
LCCN: 2016900229
Printed in the United States of America

Miracle of the Loaves and Fish ®

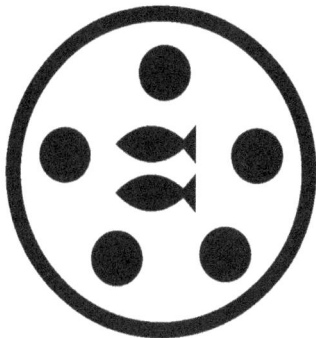

This logo is a representation of the
Miracle of the Five Loaves and Two Fish
based on the scripture Matthew 14:13-21

Miracle of the Loaves & Fish logo is a registered trademark

For apparel, jewelry, household goods and more with this
logo, go to: http://cafepress.com/miracleofloavesnfish

Miracle of the Loaves and Fish ® Shop
Expect a miracle - -everyday!
Matthew 14:13-21

Dedication

This book is personally dedicated to each person who picks it up to read. To the whole world around the globe, to people of every nation, please let God change your life, just as He has changed my life.

God has tailor made this book for you. God had you in mind when He divinely inspired this wonderful and powerful book of blessings.

I pray that today, you will start your new life in Christ Jesus. Trust God. You have never felt love like this before today. Let God wake you up from a dead life of sin.

Only God can help you, you have tried all your life and could not do it. It's your day—a new day to find God's way for life.

Acknowledgements

I give all credit and glory to God because He is the power who inspired this book. Thank you Lord for creating this awesome book.

Special Thanks To:

My Son-in-Law Marc Dobbs and my daughter LaShawn Dobbs. Thank you for the support, encouraging faith and love. You have great rewards in heaven and on the earth.

Pastor Frank & Ergie Boddie, together you have shined a light of love in my life—I thank God for you both.

Table of Contents

Introduction

The Vision of Wisdom

Holy Inspired by God
Volume II

Introduction

The Vision of Wisdom is Holy Inspired by God. God speaks according to His Word that has already been written (The Holy Bible). He will not speak anything contrary to His already written Word. Every word that is written in The Vision of Wisdom is in sync with God's already written Word.

Before reading, pray and ask God to give you knowledge and understanding of what you're about to read. Without seeking God first, these words of wisdom will not make sense to the carnal mind.

The Word of God speaks of this in **1 Corinthians 2:14 (NLT)** But people who aren't spiritual can't receive these truths from God's Spirit. It all sounds foolish to them and they can't understand it, for only those who are spiritual can understand what the Spirit means.

God has been revealing 'The Vision of Wisdom' to me over the last twelve years, (2003-2015). I sought Him and asked Him for wisdom and He did just that. This book is Volume II of III.

There is much that I do understand and then there are some that I, myself, still have not received the wisdom to understand exactly what God is saying, but as I continue to read and seek Him, He grants me more understanding of what He is saying.

Therefore, I encourage you to seek God. Ask God for knowledge, wisdom and understanding. In the book of James; **James 1:5 (NLT)** it is written "If you need wisdom, ask our generous God, and he will give it to you. He will not rebuke you for asking."

After you pray and ask God for knowledge, wisdom and understanding, believe that He has heard you and by faith receive, because that's what you asked Him for.

As you read The Vision of Wisdom, allow the words of wisdom to minister to your heart and mind. Don't try to figure it out carnally, if there's something you read that you don't understand, ask God for understanding.

There were several times God has given me a phrase and the next sentence or sometimes a couple days later, He would give me what seemed like the same phrase all over again, but once I went back and read the two phrases I realized, though they were alike they were not totally the same. At first I could not understand why God was repeating Himself, just in a different manner.

He then let me know—we learn by repetition, the more we hear or read something it will take root in us. Hence, His reason for doing this is because He is depositing His wisdom in us, not wisdom from man, but He is depositing His wisdom in us as we take in His words.

I know that 'The Vision of Wisdom: Holy Inspired by God Volume II' will bless you just as it has blessed me, because these words are Holy Inspired by God, this wisdom is not of my own, but from Him.

As you read, you too will know that the mind of man could not fathom what God is saying, therefore it had to come from Him. Thank God for a spiritual mind to understand the things of the spirit!

The vision of wisdom is wisdom for your vision.

It takes God's vision to see into God's wisdom.

When you have the Fruit of the Spirit you will see the physical fruit in your life.

When you have the Fruit of the Spirit you will see the spiritual fruit.

Some people you have to resist in order to resist the devil in them.

Don't let your mistakes be your brakes.

There are snakes in the grass and these snakes wear a mask.

There are snakes in the grass and there are snakes in your paths.

Your bad seeds can harm you because they travel into the future.

Your past is the past when you leave it in the past.

A gift from the heart is your heart that's the gift.

When you plan your future remember the wisdom from your past.

If you want to learn about reaping you have to first learn about sowing.

Some people want God's light, but not God's life.

Ignorance is blind, but the truth can see.

When you cheat to reap you reap cheap.

Obedience is a seed it's the seed of obedience.

You have to sow obedience to reap obedience from heaven.

When you are heavenly wise you are heavenly smarter then earth.

Generosity is a great philosophy, but the best philosophy is God.

Magic is a false direction to deception.

Ungrateful never learns the word thankful.

Your mind was designed to operate with God's mind.

God will help your mind think beyond your mind.

Your mind was designed for a heavenly mind.

God sowed miracles in you that you can reap through Jesus.

Alcohol is the devil's nectar—it will twist your mind to believe his lecture.

The mouth is an amazing enemy—you will eat what it speaks.

If God gives you a boat you should know it will float.

The devil wants to destroy your brain because in your brain you hear God's name.

When you were born sin made you cry at birth.

Confirmation is information.

The sign of a new mind is the light that shines.

When God breaks chains he breaks demonic claims.

Never claim a chain—dis-claim it.

There is no border when you are out of order.

You need a seed to seed a need.

When you are saved the devil's your slave.

Hell has many doors, but heaven has one.

A liar's tongue never won.

A lie is bondage and lies are bondages.

Faith is like a servant ready to serve you.

You sow what God sowed and you share what God shared.

Attentiveness is readiness—when you are attentive you are ready to listen.

Faith is the substance to get you whatever you ask for —in God's will.

There's a difference between being mad or being wicked.

Obedience is good works.

Faith is a positive force with positive power.

Faith moves the spiritual into the natural realm and moves the natural into the spiritual realm

We cannot divorce our flesh, but we can divorce our flesh from walking in the flesh.

It is good to be in the word, but it is better for the word to be in you too.

Satan is like a ventriloquist—he uses us like dummies.

If you truly pay attention you will truly remember more.

Who can forget when thinking? Who can remember without thinking?

Your mind cannot wander when you ponder.

An attentive hearer helps many people.

When you are doing everything God wants you to do, then God can do everything in His will for you.

Your passions enhance your memory.

Some people say, "God don't care." Then breath the air He shares.

God will make you think beyond what you think.

When you're rich some people don't want to know you—they want to know your money.

Sinful memories are your enemies.

Obedience follows righteousness, disobedience follows sin.

To be free is like a log drifting at sea.

Every time you believe the enemy you become your enemy.

Faith is a positive force that does not force you.

It's called freewill because you're will is free.

A forced will, wills to be free. A forced will is not your will.

When your focus is off your memory's off. When your focus is on your memory's on.

Another day another way.

You are lied to before every sin.

Wisdom learns from everyone.

A man fights toe to toe, but the coward fights toe to heel.

Denial is not a river.

Sometimes in the church they will fish for men and after they catch them they will throw them back.

Denial, is not like a river that flows freely.

Integrity is like life and when it's gone—it's like death.

Speaking is sowing, too. When you speak you sow, you reap what you speak

Even a duck don't believe in luck.

Let it go before it grows.

A Christian's memory should be the devils enemy.

When you are out of control you are powerless, when you are in control you are powerful.

Faults start with negative thoughts.

Running is a defense—running could save your life.

Running is a defense—running saved many lives.

Running is a defense—even animals know that.

When you prove that your word means nothing then what can you get by your word.

A true friend wont mistreat you, owe you money and cheat you.

To see God in a person, you have to see God's fruit.

True Christian's don't burn bridges they build them.

A liar fears the truth—when he should fear the lies.

When you don't let it go, you make it grow.

Even an animal can be nice before it attacks you.

Solutions are problems fixed.

You have to work together to be together.

Evil knows the ways to Hell.

God has a seed for whatever you need.

Sowing is a system.

When you forgive, then God will forgive you for not forgiving.

A good seed in the ground, will help turn things around.

When you treat your enemies kindly it will make them feel guilty.

If you have a friend name misery, you need to lose his company.

Alcohol is a dangerous thing, it will twist the mind as it kills the brain.

A liar has two tongues and they both tell lies.

A liar's mouth is never hungry for the truth.

People are everything that God isn't, but Jesus makes people everything that God is.

Honesty is not the enemy and evil motives is a cobra.

A person who complains even complains about other people who complain.

A finger at other people's faults will not change your mistakes.

The Spirit of God is here to make more people of God.

Having patience with God does not mean have patience with sinning.

Negativity is a demonic activity.

When you sin, it leaves a stain that can be seen in the spiritual realm—which extends into the eyes of the physical realm.

Meat isn't meat when you make it weak, only a baby eats already chewed meat.

How can a Christian walk if he doesn't stand? Don't you have to stand up to walk?

Some interpretations are abominations.

Anger is the weakness that weak people cannot control.

An argument wants to be strong, an argument wants to control.

Arguments are the weakest conversations.

How can you sow when you hold what you're supposed to sow?

Anger is danger.

If you focus on people's ways you can lose your way.

The things you say are the things you'll pay.

People who are mad win the race for anger.

Negativity calls the devil and says "I'm over here."

Love is never an enemy, but it rules **OVER** <u>EVERY</u> enemy.

Enemies come in many colors, but the **darkest** enemy is the worst.

God uses the stars as a sign, they tell you the storm is over!

NEWSFLASH:
There is no sin that exists without temptation and there is no temptation that exists without sin.

NEWSFLASH:
Don't make a god of worldly things—you cannot bring them to hell.

Patience comes with practice, that is why we must practice patience.
You can tell if a person loves God—by their obedience.

> ***Obedience is obvious***
> ***Obedience is evidence***
> ***Obedience is obvious evidence***

Robbery is the enemy of charity.

When temptation tries to tempt you, you are not sinning if you're not tempted.

Temptation exists from sin and temptation exists to sin.

God tests without temptation, the devil tests with temptation.

Temptation comes from sin and temptation is not your friend.

Sin is like a hook and temptation is like bait.

Spiritual sight comes from God's insight.

Temptation is from the devil and temptation is for the devil.

God doesn't use temptations, but He will use the one who uses temptations.

A liar practices lying and he never gets good.

NEWSFLASH:
Fleshy eyes are not wise, fleshy eyes do tell lies.

NEWSFLASH:
The more you help people the more people help you.

NEWSFLASH:
The flesh is the addiction that only Christians have the power to break.

Faith is the key that unlocks the unimaginable beyond the earthly imaginations.

Just like the earth turns, your life can turn , but faster…

Only God can be on your inside and your outside at the same time.

God is the infinity source of life—which means life always existed because the forever existence of God.

Life always existed because God's life always existed.

Some people walk in their own religions of sin—what they believe in their own mind.

The education of this world you die without. The education of God's kingdom you die within.

No respecter of persons means to love people in different religions too.

Everything old is old and everything that looks new is old—this is not a mystery.

It is better to forgive before an apology—it shows more love than waiting on an apology.

Everywhere you see holiness you can spiritually see God there. Everywhere you see evil you can spiritually see the devil there.

Just like holiness is never away from God—sin is never away from the devil.

The devil wants to get a foothold through where you're trying to get a prayer to.

The devil wants you to sin-away with him.

When God says take a left turn , don't take a right. When God says take a right turn , don't take a left.

How can God teach you how to think when you follow what you think?

How can you be where you're supposed to be following someone who cannot see?

If you are not thinking faith—you are not thinking. The devil knows that sin harms us, that's why he wants us to sin.

Every time we sin we hurt ourselves—*sin sows pain.*

The way of the wise is quenching and refreshing, but the way of the wicked is dehydratingly dry.

The largest clock on earth is the earth.

Greed is a hungry existence—it's belly is like the bottomless pit.

Every time we sin we hurt ourself with pain because sin reaps pain.

Sin sows in pain and reaps in pain.

You can control what you sow—when you sow the Word in FAITH through CHRIST.

Sometimes when you sow sin it looks like pleasure until it grows.

People who act out of control—it's because they don't have any control.

Sin effects the seen and unseen not just the physical world.

A person who cannot control anything tries to control every little thing.

You have to have faith to sow in faith—you have to have faith to faithfully sow.

Evil is ugly—there is nothing beautiful about evil.

Time spent is time meant.

When everything goes—there goes everything.

The only gift you can give God is yourself back to God.

Sue with righteousness, not with revenge.

You either love sinning more than you love yourself or love yourself more than sinning.

All candy isn't sweet some candy is sour.

It is a sin to forget your brother and buy from another.

Every crime that people commit is also who the devil is.

If you give your life to God, then God can give your life back to you.

If you walk in sin you work in sin.

God wants **ALL** of you—a LITTLE won't do.

Ask God to "Help me Lord to live Your Word."

Satan is a liar, if you follow him you are a liar also.

To agree with disobedience is to disagree with righteousness.

If you curse and swear that's the devil.

Cursing and swearing inside your mind first, then you reveal it secondly.

True forgiveness shows and shares.

I love you to life—not to death.

Whatever you do to commit sin is what you did—not Adam.

God speaks nonexistence into existence because existence is in His voice.

There exists things of the Spirit deeper than your thinking.

The man that wandereth out of the way of understanding shall remain in the congregation of the dead. **Proverbs 21:16**

Who you project is who you reflect.

Exercise is you investing into your health.

Do not err my beloved brethern. **James 1:16**

My dear brothers and sisters, if someone among you wanders away from the truth and is brought back, [20] you can be sure that whoever brings the sinner back from wandering will save that person from death and bring about the forgiveness of many sins. **JAMES 5:19-20 (NLT)**

Faith frees, fear deceives.

We are born into a wave of sin—which surrounds and engulfs us into a sea called the world.

To follow Christ you must follow God's word.

Regarding the Bible:
Don't take what YOU think you need, take it all. God said it all because we need it ALL.

God's time in your life should be all the time, because if it wasn't for God you wouldn't have no time.

God's Word is God's mind manifested for your mind to be healed.

Whenever you commit sin you are separating yourself away from God Himself.

God's will is "THE WAY."

The bible is God's nature—it shares who God is.

If you give to receive—you give to deceive.

Faith is like dynamite and obedience lights the wick.

Faith explodes into action by you activating obedience.

Only the saved behave.

Jesus is the only basket I can put all my eggs in.

When you allow sin—at that pint you had to agree with the devil's mind.

Prove your walk by walking in proof.

Is the devil really your enemy or your friend? It depends on what you do and who you obey.

If you are a new creation—stop acting like the old creation.

Christ is the medication for every situation.

Take what you need when it fits what God needs from you.

When a person commits sin they personalize it to fit their lifestyle.

The "will" of sin is to arrange a deranged lifestyle for your life.

Disobedience is the beginning of self-destruction which ends in spiritual destruction.

Disobedience works in the direction towards hell.; obedience works in the direction towards heaven.

Your disobedience empowers satan's power against you.

The beginning of disobedience is the end of obedience.

Disobedience works in the direction towards death.

The devil knows that your mind is a weapon—it can be used for him or against him.

When you commit sin—your mind and satan's mind come together as one mind on the same accord against your mind to destroy your mind...***Now That's Deceit!***

Obedience works in the direction of life.

The devil's mind works to trick your mind against yourself.

If you are a sheep—why are you roaring like a lion?

Let God make you—who HE made you.

When you are righteous—you are just.

When you are not God's tool—you are the devil's fool.

When God speak—LEAP!

IN CHRIST:
When you let go—you GROW!

When you let sin in, troubles begin.

Whatever God gives you to do, HE will do it for HIS glory.

When you pick up your bible, it will pick you **UP**!

Jesus is the way—that's why we obey.

What God says once is forever.

Always pray while the devil speaks.

Faith thinks before it acts—fear acts before it thinks.

When you're out of your mind you can't figure out what's wrong with your mind.

Prove your walk by walking in truth.

God wants to transform us out of what the world deformed us into.

Life is good when you're good and life is bad when you are bad.

Obedience wouldn't matter if it did not matter, but it matters to God.

Once saved always saved is not true—if you forsake God.

Obedience moves you closer to heaven. Disobedience moves you closer to hell.

To work for the devil is to work against yourself.

Obedience speaks louder than speech.

Obedience speaks love out loud to God.

Are you walking in complaints or walking in thanks?

In Christ

The higher you GROW *the deeper you* GROW

If you don't deny yourself you're following yourself —not Christ.

If it's not in Christ—what people think can make you sink.

Sometimes God takes away—to keep us on the right way.

Being born-again: if you're not trying, you are lying.

When people hurt you—don't hurt people too.

When you commit sin against the Kingdom of Heaven—you commit sin for the kingdom of hell.

A light bulb gets brighter and brighter as you get closer and closer, but it gets darker and darker as you get further and further.

There is nothing on earth more valuable than heaven.

If you step out of your square, you will step into another sphere—in Christ.

If you are looking for love in mankind you are looking for love in the wrong places.

Let your works speak for you—not against you.

Obedience use what God says use, and lose what God says lose.

Heaven's happy right now because heaven's always happy!

Prove you worship God in your walk—then you can worship in your talk.

Your walk proves your talk—in Christ.

Your talk can lie, but your walk can't lie.

It's impossible to fall short in Christ because HIS righteousness isn't short in me.

Cursing comes back to curse you.

Blessings comes back to bless you.

Cursing is rehearsing the devil's conversing.

If you speak perverse you rehearse the worse.

Sheep don't howl, but liars do.

When you read your bible to learn—that's labor you earn.

When Christians agree—devils flee.

When you allow sin—troubles begin.

Whatever God enables you to do, you are able to do for God.

A warship can't worship God—don't be a warship.

The thoughts of God are a diamond mine.

You can be vice or have the mind of Christ.

You're either vice or with Christ.

Always put God first—FIRST!

When you are not God's tool, you are the devils fool.

In God's hand—we can stand.

Only God can make what's invisible—visible.

Comprehension is not a new invention.

If you're afraid of fire you should be afraid of sin.

There is a lesson before your blessing.

Live to help and not to hurt.

Whatever you sow has to grow—whether good or bad.

God pollinates good seed, satan pollinates bad seed.

In Christ every tear drop counts.

You cannot walk like Christ arguing with devils.

Pride is not a reward—it's a sickness.

Did you know that you cannot love God without obedience?

God only invests in good sowing.

You obeyed the devil with ALL your heart. Why obey God with half your heart.

The righteous live clean, but the unrighteous unclean.

Hope calls God for help.

Keep on believing and receiving—it's when you stop believing you stop receiving.

If you're not different, you're not innocent.

If you give the devil enough rope, he will hang you with it.

My will is perfect, only when it lines up with God's Word.

We all have sinned— before Christ, not after Christ.

We all were sinners, but some are now ex-sinners.

The devil wants us to focus on what we've lost.

God wants us to focus on what HE won.

God wants to be used by the righteous.

Christ is God showing us Himself.

Make God your highlight and you'll live a high life.

Conquer desperation with God's inspiration.

In Christ we can endure this war for sure.

If you decide to climb God's mountain, don't slip on the devil's slope.

You cannot make logical decisions with illogical thoughts.

There is no reason for a man to be unreasonable.

There is no stinking in Godly thinking.

The only way that you can lose is if you lose "***The Way.***"

Don't focus on what people do to you, focus on what God does for you.

To conform to the Word is to transform—to perform for the Word.

God can change the devil's mess around to bless.

When you are walking in Christ—you will talk like Christ.

You will have faith when you believe.

When you fight the good fight of faith you knockout unbelief.

When you think defeated, the devil has succeeded.

No matter where you are—Jesus is where you are.

What sin conforms, God can transform.

Actions speak volume.

Seeking the Lord is seeking to live.

A Christian can make every thought obey God.

Faith never thinks negative thoughts.

Faith never says "I cannot obey God all the time."

What Adam gave away—Christ gave back your way.

If sin still has power over you—you're still dead.

The sins that you commit many Christians have rejected, so it's not impossible to quit.

If your mouth is not pure, your heart is not pure yet.

Jesus was born in the flesh so we can be born in the Spirit.

God's love fits everybody's hand like a glove.

God does not speak temporal, HE speaks eternal.

In life you have two different times, there's God's time and there's—God's time.

When you invest in the positive you defeat the negative.

Jesus was born dying so that we could be born living.

We all might slip, but we don't have to fall.

Faith never sleeps, it's always ready to work with you.

To find out who God is, is to find out who you are.

It's impossible to have the mind of satan and the mind of Christ too.

Sinners do not have the Fruit of the Spirit.

Put God in ALL your thoughts and ALL your thoughts will be Godly.

God's power is our power.

The devil doesn't care if you read the bible—as long as you're NOT a DOER.

Christ will help the cursed become blessed.

When God is IN you, you're IN love.

If your life is in the Lord then the Lord is in your life.

Positivity **ALWAYS** wins over negativity.

Negative talk is pollution, not a positive solution.

Only God can change your night to day and your darkness to light.

One of the weapons the devil use against us is us.

A finger pointed is not a hand of help.

It is better to encourage then to discourage.

An argument takes the energy away from the target meant.

Just because you have a target does not mean you'll always hit bulls eye.

Blame always introduces shame.

A master mind is a mind that is mastered by God.

When love is in your life then your life is in love.

Communication promotes cooperation.

You have to want the best for yourself, then live the best for God.

On God's Word ponder and your thoughts will not wander.

You should not be running to hell, you should be running from hell.

There is no job too **BIG** or small for God.

Don't let your pride be your guide—let God guide you.

You can kill a lie with the truth, but you cannot kill the truth with a lie.

When the devil attacks you—stop attacking people.

You cannot act like a devil and be with God—even the devil know that.

For every time you use the truth, the devil cannot use a lie.

The truth is a weapon against the devil's lies.

Do not play with the devil or his friends—if you are wise.

A new creation cannot be an old sinner—still.

Christians, if Gods' Word you ponder, you will not wonder.

As long as you're on God's side, you're on the winning side.

With Christ your needs are completed, without Christ your needs are defeated.

It does not matter what the devil says—only what God says.

Your behavior shows sinners if you're real or just like them.

God's Spirit helps you to obey HIS spirit.

You cannot be in Christ obeying outside of Christ.

If you have wisdom you have no pride—wisdom comes when pride leaves.

Obedience makes you happy, disobedience makes you sad.

A fool walks in foolishness and a wise man's tongue is never dumb.

The breath of God is the life of man.

Life is a crisis without Christ.

The breath of God is the breath of man.

Either you are on offense or defense, but you cannot be on the fence.

Evil is the sickness that only God's love can heal.

Evil is the practice of the unwise because a wise man will not practice evil.

Repentance is not a game to practice the same sin relentless.

Fasting fights against your flesh.

A reckless tongue stops your faith and destroys your prayer results.

Faith speaks faith, if you're not speaking faith its not faith.

Your past and your present can make your future wiser.

The mind goes in many different directions, but in reality focus on corrections.

To keep your mind in check you have to check your mind.

Love is the fruit that carries all the fruit.

Don't forget all fruit have seeds, even the Fruit of the Spirit.

The Fruit of the Spirit is for sowing seeds of the fruit.

A dog is a wonderful animal, but God is a man's best friend.

God spelled backwards is dog—guess who twisted that.

Fatih and fear cannot share.

Only the faithful are lawful.

People who live to love—love to live.

When you have God, God has you!

If you follow a fool, you will fall.

Only with God you can live Godly.

Obedience keeps your connection to God strong.

Who God call saints are not sinners—He knows the difference.

God has a plan for you, that's why HE planned you!

Obey everyday and the Lord will pay.

Obedience all day keeps the devil away.

When the devil try to play, show him it's God you obey.

As long as you curse you will always be cursed.

When it's God you fear, you spiritually hear.

When God you fear, HIS love you share.

If you can't show me the way, you don't now the way.

Some people talk like light, but act like night.

If your affections are set below—rest your affections above.

If God is on the inside good works are on the outside.

If the devil is on the inside, bad works are on the outside.

Every time you sin the devil wins.

The devil doesn't mind proud preaching that's complicated—it's the simplified preaching that intensifies his anger.

The devil is afraid of his own fear because when you pray he gets scared.

When the devil throw fear at you, you throw faith back at him.

A true sheep will never behave as a wolf.

Fear is afraid of prayer.

You can reverse the devils weapon of fear, as a weapon against him—called prayer.

Christians share God's righteousness to be righteous.

True regeneration brings change and reformation.

True repentance is followed by removing faults with God's help.

True repentance will give you new desires to give up bad behaviors.

Where there's no reformation there's no regeneration.

God's focus is on your problems so you don't have to.

God can take care of your problems, He doesn't need your help—just your faith.

Only the meek really seek.

Learn to be the bible not just read the bible.

The Holy Spirit of obedience wants you to obey Him, so He empowers you with the power to obey.

If you work the Word, the Word will work in you.

The devil retrieves your power by deceiving it from you.

When the devil deceives Christians into negative thinking he has deceived you against yourself.

The only way the devil can hurt you is by you becoming negative.

Your actions speak louder than memorizing bible scriptures.

Before you judge—judge to love.

Do not be the victim of disobedience—become the victor of obedience.

If you're not sure if you are saved a clue is how you act.

If you act the same you're not saved—no reborn Christian acts the same.

The Spirit who you serve on the inside will show who you serve on the outside.

Once you hold God's hand, He will never let it go.

False Christians live like they're God's boss—God will show them who's boss in the end.

Disobedience to God's will shows hate not love.

If you want a future, make a future.

If I am the righteousness of God, how can I be in the iniquity of Adam still?

Your obedience brings God pleasure.

Faith is the substance to get you whatever you desire —in God's will.

Faith waits on obedience to work.

Salvation: You cannot lose it, but you can leave it.

There is faith in righteousness because you have to have faith to be righteous.

If you sleep with the devil you'll keep birthing sin.

Obedience will help your faith to help you.

Obedience helps faith work.

If you act the same, you are the same, but if you act different, you are changed.

What God wants for you is the only thing you need to want.

Faith never behaves negatively.

Faith moves the spiritual into the natural.

Faith with works is never dead.

The more you practice obedience the easier it is to obey God.

The devil is a smart ventriloquist—he always finds a dummy.

Hardship seeks friendship with God.

If the Angels can fall anyone can fall, freewill never stops giving choices.

Are you born again or dead again?

God test for obedience, the devil tempts for disobedience.

When you do things right, right things happen. When you do things wrong, wrong things happen.

We are not born again away from freewill. We are born again with freewill. We still have a choice, God will not force you to go to heaven.

For the devil to have power over a Christian, he know he has to make you weak.

Faith obeys nothing but the truth.

To misbehave is to walk enslaved.

We ALL must die. Why not die for Christ?

How can I be a sinner when I have been crucified with Christ and I no longer live?

If you let the devil get into your mind your decisions belong to him.

We don't walk by feelings we walk by faith.

If you want prosperity, practice generosity.

You cannot live right hanging with the wrong people.

A man without God is like a fish without water—dead.

God makes a way out of no way—because He is THE WAY!

Without obedience there is no light because obedience shows light.

If you do not communicate with God how can you cooperate with Him?

Hesitation is the beginning of procrastination.

Wisdom has vision.

Where there's no light there is no life.

A lie seeks negative thoughts.

Share love and not pride—there's no love in pride.

If you live like you're in heaven now, you will be in heaven later. If you live like you're in hell now, you will be in hell later.

The way you live now will determine where you'll live later.

God wants to fill your cup till it overflows. The devil wants to steal your cup.

We are not omnipresent, we are God present. We are all with God at the same time.

Without fellowship we are a sinking ship in Christ.

If you want everything you see, you will never see God.

Sometimes when God opens a door we close it.

You have to stop making your past your future. Make your future a better past.

Right and wrong are like east and west—they are far apart.

You cannot live like a devil and be a saint.

Love always builds up, hate always tear's down.

Never look up to satan look down on him.

Love will guide you, hate will force you.

You can lead a horse to water, but you cannot make him read his bible.

You can't talk your walk, you have to walk your walk.

How much bible you know doesn't mean you're at a high level—it means you study.

We all have sin, but the righteous have rule over theirs.

If it quacks like a duck—it's a duck. If you talk like a sinner—you're a sinner.

Anything you can think of—and beyond that, that's what God can do!

Fast talkers think that if they can talk faster than you can think then they can fool you.

It is better to be with God with no friends than without God with many friends.

God wants to have a love to love relationship with you.

When God is in your heart, He is on your side.

When God is on the inside He fights devils on the outside for you.

If you walk in the Spirit your flesh cannot win.

Some Christians put God last and expect Him to put them first.

A liar is a coward of the truth.

Jesus died for our sins, so we can die from our sins.

If you want to see what God can do show God what you can do.

Your mouth exposes your thoughts.

The small things can show the greatest humility.

When you limit what you believe you limit what you receive.

It's more valuable for people to see that you're a Christian than for you to say you're a Christian.

The mouth will expose the maturity of ones mind.

If everybody like you, you're doing something wrong.

A person's mouth can be a sign of weakness.

When you can't ever be wrong, God cannot show what is right through you.

Evidence of our Creator is creation.

When you talk to a person that will not listen—you listen.

If you never stop asking you'll never stop learning.

Some people may be around your life—that doesn't mean they're in your life.

If you fall down, bow down.

The truth can heal what a lie can steal.

If your mind's in the past—your future is behind you.

Obey what God says and He will bless your day.

A lie hurts more than telling the truth.

The reward for being wrong is learning right.

God's will wants your will to be His.

Holiness is like a chisel—it chips away sin.

Some Christians have been lied to so long by the devil, they have a hard time believing the truth.

When you give your life to God, God will give His life to you.

Faith works when you use works.

Lies without guilt come for an unclean heart.

Satan hurts, God helps.

If you know God's voice—you also know the devil's voice.

Some people talk so much that they talk in their sleep too.

We don't need to pray everyday—just every moment.

Sometimes righteous words make sinners ashamed to speak.

Do you have enough unrighteousness in you to feel uncomfortable around sin?

It doesn't matter where you live, only who lives in you—in Christ.

Being nice is nice, but being holy is holiness.

The word right is in righteous.

The person who wins the argument is the person who stops talking first.

When faith loses love—it dies.

Whatever God is—the devil is not.

If you want to become strong—become strong in the Lord.

We cannot pay God, but we CAN obey God!

Why sinners don't believe in heaven?...If life happened once it's not impossible to happen again. Anything that happens one time always happens again.

If you put God last—you won't last.

A man without God is like lungs without air.

Be enslaved to behave.

If you are not walking like Christ you are walking like the enemy.

Talk is cheap if you can't prove God in your walk.

Walking into a church does not mean you are saved —walking like Christ means you're saved.

Any behavior opposite of the Bible means you are walking and operating in lies.

Are you a willing lamb to suffer or a roaring lion to fight?

Does your walk equal your talk?

Practice telling the truth and not lying.

A Christians friend should never destroy his friendship with God.

God loves you. Do you love God?

A Christian should choose friends that love God—if they desire a greater relationship.

It's good to be friendly without being friends with the wicked.

Friendship with the wicked is like heaven and hell being friends.

Sin and righteousness are not friends—they're enemies.

A righteous man's ways are seen, but the hypocrite's ways are shameful.

A hypocrite has two faces—one of them are false.

Greed is an addiction, some people are addicted to wanting more.

You earthly treasures are like people—they won't last.

Set your love above the things below.

When your mind is free it doesn't matter where your flesh be.

Some Christians need to practice walking more and talking less.

Without God your heart absorbs sin like a sponge absorbs water.

In Christ it doesn't matter how you die—it matters how you live.

Love treats people the way they would like to be treated.

With Jesus you don't have to gamble—you will win!

On the day of death, what is more important—What you own? or Who owns your soul?

Forget hocus-pocus—make God your focus.

When you memorize the scriptures, memorize obeying them.

A Christian has many storms on the outside, but the sun always shines on the inside.

The human heart beats closer to death with every beat.

The devil never pays—he always steals.

It is better to tell the truth and make man mad than to lie and make God mad.

God can take the place of anything, but there's nothing that can take the place of God.

Pride says "Everybody has to be like me."

Success starts with God.

Why is it easier to insult people than to compliment them?

Brothers don't live by what you feel then you'll let the devil steal.

God is fair and He loves to share.

Your words say who you are and what you are.

My pleasure is bringing pleasure to God.

If people would tell the truth as much as they lie they would be perfect.

If you're not in prison on the inside you are free on the outside.

When God speaks the universe waits to obey him.

The greatest weapon against ignorance is intelligence.

When sad think your way happy in the Lord.

When you're sad pray till you're happy.

It doesn't matter how much you have when you have God.

In everything negative there's a positive side.

If you really want to change be with people that are changing.

Don't ever cry over spilled milk, just ask God for another cup.

Christians can speak their lives into correction.

Always pray while the devil talks.

Don't let your body be your boss.

If you let the devil look down at you, you will be under his feet.

The beginning of sin is weak thoughts.

There's something wrong with your walk when God didn't ordain your talk.

If you say, "I'm a Christian," and sin day and night, it's a good thing you sleep—you need rest.

The less you sin, the more you win.

Love listens, hate ignores.

When you open your bible don't just read—listen.

People say, "Get a life." You cannot get a life without The Way, The Truth and The Life in your life.

Every time you lie you help the devil…Why?

No matter how much good you giveaway, you will never run out.

When you have God you have everything God has.

Let God control your mind that He designed.

The words you speak did God choose them?

The only now who agrees with everything you say is you.

Some people want everything their way, but life is not our way it's God's way.

If you want to hear a lie—don't ask an honest man.

Avoid every delusion that comes against your vision.

The proud becomes angry when you disagree, but the humble stays calm.

Obeying is the beginning of growing.

Don't allow what you own, own you.

God teach me to be humble and meek, to hold my tongue when I should not speak.

The sun always shines—even when it storms, so can you.

Real faith waits on God's time.

We all sin, but we all don't mean to.

The grass looks greener on the other side—until you see that person's other side.

The devil will use fear to try to stop your faith.

The devil uses delusion for confusion.

Faith is the beginning of positive thinking.

If you're not saved—you life is hell to pay.

Look at the Bible to see your image.

If you're driving towards God—don't back up.

When God rings your doorbell—don't be a dumbbell.

Be thankful, live grateful.

Only God's wisdom is full of God's vision.

Hide your pride where you cannot find it.

With adversity, sorrow and pain—this wicked heart I must tame.

If you are not walking right—get out of my light.

The vision of wisdom is wisdom full of vision.

When you sin you're being selfish because you sin for yourself.

Just because we were born dead doesn't mean we have to stay dead.

We try and fail, but God's righteousness will always prevail.

Out of confessions come blessings with God.

Some people claim to be Christians, but they sin like they invented it and have a patent.

How can you be the light of the world walking in the darkness of the world?

We are sealed by accepting God and condemned by rejecting God.

Your fruit is for everyone, so share.

If you hang with sinners you don't hate sin.

If you work for God he'll work with you.

If you feed a wicked man he will eat from your hand.

A lifestyle of intentional sins is a lifestyle of intentional separation from God.

Saying "I'm only flesh." Is saying, "I have no choice, I have to sin."

We were all sinners, but some have been changed into saints.

If I am a believer and sinner still, I would be unequally yoked against myself.

There is no faith in filth.

Your obedience proves your belief in God.

You can love your enemies, but you don't have to live with them.

Only godly living is living for God.

If you are saved, you don't have to obey sin, sin has to obey you.

Only the dense will straddle the fence.

Where there is magic, there is deceit.

Remember, when you ask God for things—He controls the time.

When God speaks—even the devil has to listen.

We were made innocent for God and Jesus was made guilty for us.

If you play with the devil, you will get burnt.

If you really want to taste life—taste God.

God loves you. Do you act like you love Him?

Where there's humility there's tranquility.

If you focus on being right with heaven—you'll be right with earth too.

Christians are God's power outlets—for sinners to plug in and find light.

Obey to habitual obedience.

When you speak the Word some people get mad—because the devil's mad in them.

There is provision in your vision.

Some people don't want you to have an opinion, but God does—that's why He gave you one.

Humility brings tranquility.

The devil cannot argue against the Word because the Word casts down arguments.

Faith never strikes out, FAITH hits HOME RUNS!

What things may seem like they are—sometimes they are not.

Life's a vacation—in Christ.

Pain reminds us of sin daily.

If you're never convicted—you are not elected.

Jesus was not our sacrifice for disobedience—He had to be obedient too.

At the Cross, Jesus did not turn His back on you. Will you turn your back on Him?

God's Word…we can get it wrong, but God still said it's right.

The righteous should fight in the Spirit only, never in the flesh.

It takes light to speak light.

You cannot always control what comes into your mind, but you can control what comes out of your mouth.

Love is the only shield that hate cannot penetrate.

An evil man can talk as warm as the summer, but his heart is as cold as the winter.

In life you have to have a goal—to get the gold.

Only you can control the door of your heart—who you will let enter and live there.

Man can make snowflakes, but only God can make real snowflakes.

Life isn't about what's fair unto you, life is about what you do that's fair unto God.

Good works cannot satisfy, but when God sees your will and your works it allows God to keep you satisfied.

Your brain is not only to think, it's also a frequency receiver and transmitter.

Why worry about anything when you have the God of everything.

Greed has BIG eyes and see everything but the Lord.

People don't want to neglect themselves—they rather neglect other people.

God knows we have to go through the worst in this life to become the best in both life.

We are blessed in every breath—so breathe!

Just because you go to church does not mean you are the church.

Anybody can be hateful, but only a few are faithful.

It takes a brave man to admit he's afraid.

If God is in you—miracles will come out of you.

Don't let youth fool you—death is seeking the young too.

Jesus obey God—are you better than Him?

If you want everything God has for you—put God in everything.

God made the sun and moon to agree with the earth.

Don't ever grow out of crying to the Lord—we are His children.

Pride hides tears and destroys prayers.

We all have visions and watching television is not your vision.

Jesus' obedience is an example for us to follow.

With God—one man can change the future.

If Jesus followed obedience all the way to heaven— you follow obedience all the way to heaven.

God put everything He needs in you for pleasure.

Hate never obeys, but love always obeys who he loves.

When you do what God wants—you won't have to hunt for what you want.

If you want a blessing, let your life be a blessing to others.

True love never obeys hate and hate never obeys true love.

Jesus did not come here for us to sin, He came here for us not to sin.

When you really love God—the people you lose weren't friends.

With God—the one who knows a little and obeys it all, is better than the one who knows a lot and obeys a little.

If you live like the devil you're gonna go through hell.

All will remember the bible in hell and believe it.

A child's temper controls him, but a man controls his temper.

It profits nothing to be smart in knowledge and dumb in obedience.

If you put on faith—you'll be safe.

Life isn't how much you have—it's how much you give.

When you control your temper, you can control the temper of those who can't.

If you want to eat the good of the land, you have to obey the Lord of the land.

Even though you're a mess—don't give up.

People who want to control you— can't even control themselves.

If I say I hate sin, I won't hang around sinners, sinning around me.

Some people who are out of control try to control others.

The word snitch was invented to hide evil.

Don't play with God—pray with God.

Let your flesh step down and your faith step up!

If your heart is wrong, your direction is wrong. If your heart is right your direction is right.

If you follow Jesus, He will lead you into the promised land.

Problems come, but the best part is—they go!

If you are still fighting in the flesh—you are not a faith fighter.

It's impossible to be loyal to yourself if you're not loyal to God. God gives you the power to be loyal to yourself.

Some weak Saints want the strong Saints to live sinful too.

The devil uses the weak Saints to attack the strong Saints—at times.

If you're not thankful for what you have, you can lose it.

If you respect the devil, he will disrespect you.

If you keep attacking the devil, the devil can't keep attacking you first.

Does your walk profess what you confess?

If you don't mind being corrected, you will be resurrected.

Some people believe that if they pray, read their bible and go to church that they can sin. They will find out in hell!

I dare you to share.

If God's light is in you, it is also shinning on you.

Remembering doesn't mean pondering about your past.

When you put God in control, He puts you in control of your life.

When you use a lie as a joke—I'm sure God doesn't laugh.

The devil will tell you the battle is yours—it's not, it's the Lord's.

God will not let His children go through anything they don't need to.

The young learn what the old forget—knowledge is temporal.

In a spiritual battle; every time you use flesh—the devil wins.

God knew your past before your past knew you.

If you would just get empty, there will be room for God to fill you up.

God wants you to stop living for you and to start living for Him.

You cannot be full of this world and heaven too.

In God's vision, is your vision.

A lie is the beginning of another lie.

Is the devil feeding you, or are you eating from the Lord's table?

You cannot be full of the devil and God.

How can God renew your mind if you do not read the Word of God?

If adversity is what it takes to stay close to God—give me adversity.

We have a lot of garbage in us that stinks—let God take out the trash.

What God put in you, is for Him—first.

Everyone who says they're in Christ, are not all new creations, some walk in the old creation—still.

When the devil tries to trick you into falling, fall on your knees and pray.

Some Christians will talk like they have all the answers and later read the Bible for answers too.

Christians need to learn to stop fighting against God's help.

With the devil, there's a trick in every treat.

God is the only one who can make something bad turn out good.

In prison I went from a few years with man into eternity with God.

When self gets in the way, God gets out of the way.

There's more to life than living now and more to death than dying now.

The difference between right and wrong are like day and night.

When you think of right, think of day. When you think of wrong, think of night.

When the Holy Spirit baptized you into God, He baptized you into Himself because He is God.

When God opens windows in heaven, doors open on earth.

Faith relates, but fear deflates.

God created you to do something He planned for you to do.

The good you do today, will be good tomorrow.

Don't be so earth smart that you become spiritually dumb.

Who can you turn away from sin while you're walking in sin.

Faith says "You can," it never says "You can't."

The righteous is right when they walk in the light.

Sometimes it's better to listen to people's actions than their words because actions don't lie.

Visions are real, delusions are fake.

Some people believe that hurting others feel good—until God punishes them.

Prison life is negative, but you still have a choice to speak positive.

I'm not blessed and lowly favored. I am blessed and highly favored!

If you call yourself stupid you have already agreed and if you have already agreed—you're stupid.

Seek to be meek!

If no one in heaven talks like you, who or what makes you think you'll be the first?

Do not make your fist your faith, make your faith your fist.

God is in Jesus and He is God.

We all have sinned, but the righteous have been justified.

When people lose their respect and disrespect you—you respect God.

Some wicked give to deceive as kind.

The young think about looking good. The old think about living good.

You have to humble yourself to become humble.

God will make your mind your friend; the devil will make your mind your enemy.

Practice listening; see how long you can listen without opening your mouth.

If God is with you, failure cannot come against you.

If it looks like failure—it's not.

God knows the choice you're going to choose, before you choose your choice.

How can God have His way when you're in His way?

Anyone can live stupid and die, so why not use wisdom and live?

You cannot walk towards God's gate living in hate.

If you're in the light—act right.

You can't walk like Christ, but you can walk Christ like.

Words can punch too.

A lie hurts you can the person who trusts you.

If you're not ashamed to look me in the face and lie —I'm ashamed for you.

Refuse to let people speak your past into the present to effect your future.

God will give you new memories—much better than your old ones.

There are no surprises about faith, because faith always works.

It is better to be accused of putting God in too much than not enough.

If a person is good to you—they're good for you.

You don't have to find your way when you're in Christ, because He is The Way!

Look at your problems as steps that God gives you the power to walk up.

There is no love in lies—just deceit.

The more you do nothing, the more nothing gets done.

If "mistake" were a person—he would be blamed for everything.

Sin has no respect—it destroys all who practices it.

Do not rehearse a curse—reverse a curse.

Bad attitudes make bad friendships.

Change who you're around and the things around you will change.

Before you teach God's Word—you should keep God's Word.

Put your heart in God's hands.

Teamwork—works.

I'm rubber you're glue—whatever wrong you do to me is going to stick to you.

The Holy Spirit does not discriminate against who God uses—why do you?

It's alright to play games in life, just remember, life is not a game.

Whatever you start for God, He'll finish for you.

You can help friends and family all your life, but only God can help you at the end of your life.

What you dream today, create today.

Don't focus on what you did wrong, focus on what Jesus did right.

If you're not showing what you know, you don't know enough to show.

Lessons are blessings too.

If you want somebody to listen, it is better to write them a letter.

When people treat you mean, it's the best opportunity to prove you're nice.

A work of art is an art of work.

If you live like there's no tomorrow, you won't live tomorrow.

Let no one control your happiness with their moods and attitudes.

Nice guys finish first and bad guys finish last.

Don't let your words punish you. If they're not godly —they will.

If God chose you, let Him use you.

The devil will tell you *"I'll give you the world,"* but he cannot give you what God owns.

God designed your mind to be on Christ's time.

There are treasures in you, you just have to dig to find them.

When you learn to listen, your learn to learn.

If you seek excuses, solutions will hide.

It really doesn't matter where your flesh lives, because inside of your flesh is where you live.

I care more about what a Christian shows than what he knows.

Jealousy has no friendship.

I don't need an award for loving God, because He is my reward.

Whom God doesn't call His friends—why would I call them my friends?

When you play with sin—sin doesn't play.

Be careful what you own—that comes into your mind.

Sometimes you have to let people talk until they get tired of hearing.

Don't let your words destroy your works.

Obedience shows God that you care about your behavior.

Mistakes are accidents—decisions are chosen.

Be careful what you sing, because singing is words too.

Where there is no fruit, there's no faith.

If you let God use you—the devil won't.

If you claim God's name—don't walk like Cain.

Faith says "YOU CAN!" Fear says "You can't."

Do not trade a moment of righteousness for a moment of sin.

If you will not work for man, you'll be lazy for God also.

If you work while you're young—you can play while you're old.

One wrong decision can destroy your vision.

Always remember, you pay for what you say.

If you listen to man argue, you can listen to God speaking.

When you were conceived—sin was conceived.

If you want favor—walk in good behavior.

Sinning is not worth the shame that you suffer in the end.

Obedience is a weapon against the devil. If you want to beat the devil, just obey God.

If you want to fight against the devil—obey God.

The devil knows that your mouth is a trap—it can trap you.

Obedience defeats everything from hindering your blessings.

Jesus donated His blood for you. Will you donate your blood for Him?

In life you will pick up hitchhikers, just don't let them change your life.

The devil will have someone argue with you—while God is speaking to you.

No matter what the devil says—LOVE ANYWAY!

When You're a Christian, some of the people who helped you, don't know that God ordered them.

Now faith never waits on later flesh.

If you want God to do what He can, just obey Him so He can.

Only God can takedown walls that the devil put up.

A lying tongue is more dangerous than a gun.

Are you serving God, or your attitude?

When God paves your road, don't make any potholes.

When God works on your life, He starts in your heart.

God can bless your mess and change your mess to bless others.

Negative thoughts that come to your mind are attacks from the devil to destroy your mind.

Only the free can spiritually see.

When you obey, you run the devil away.

Speaking faith is works, because speaking is an action that works.

When you are sowing, make room for growing.

Lies come, but not by hearing the Word of God.

Positive thinking thinks the best in EVERY situation —no matter what's happening in your life.

A healthy brain is controlled by healthy thoughts only, because negative thoughts are unhealthy.

Positive thinking is righteous thinking.

Every negative thought that you receive comes from the devils thoughts.

If you want God to do ALL He can, obey Him all you can.

When you walk in pride, God hides.

Your brain was created for positive thoughts. The negative thoughts are an attack to destroy your positive mind.

The Word is a shield against negative thoughts—when you use the Word it blocks them out.

The only thing you can do about your past, is work on your future.

If you seek excuses, you won't be able to count them all.

There is relief in God's belief.

Faith is like a Salmon swimming upstream—it goes against the flow.

If your attitude is up and down, your altitude is on the ground.

A fool thinks you're weak when you don't speak—it's him that's weak.

When you start believing—fear starts leaving.

When you believe—fear leaves.

My hope is in heaven, not on earth.

Time will show you hints about your future.

An excuse it not a solution, it's a diversion.

Whatever God says—don't do anything else.

Anything else other than what God says—is sin.

Your attitude reveals your altitude.

The opposite of a solution is a diversion.

Life is a rocky road, that become smooth in Christ.

When you make God glad—you make the devil mad.

If you know your vision, don't worry about provision because it's in there.

Do not work God around your schedule—work your schedule around God.

Faith is seeing Jesus with your mind's eye—regardless of what you see with your physical eyes.

The Word of God will keep you—if you keep the Word of God.

Inventing is like baseball—everything you hit won't always be a home run.

If you are acting like a sinner—you're probably not acting.

What the devil stole, God can save—your soul.

If you are afraid to be different, you're afraid to be free.

Be wise how you spend your life—more than with your money.

If you show a lack of intelligence, you will witness unfair treatment.

Life is fake without faith.

People who say, "I need to find myself," if they didn't seek God then they're still looking.

One good seed will fix your need.

Some people get amnesia when they owe you, but they are cured when you owe them.

Fear scares afraid people—not faith people.

The best teacher lives by example.

When you argue the devil gives you help.

Life is not about how you can hurt people, it's about how you can help people.

It doesn't matter where you are if Jesus is there with you.

If you don't walk towards your goal, your goal won't walk towards you.

If you have accepted freedom on the inside, show freedom on the outside.

An inventors mind lubricates the minds of others.

It is good to seek careers, but first seek the God of careers.

The humbleness in humility is valuable to all who see.

It is good to be kind, it helps the soul shine.

If you want to be blessed, behave blessed.

Hope is destroyed by dope.

If God is in you, listen to gospel music.

To hear God, you have to listen for good.

When the covenant changed, God's Word remained.

When Christians hear good, they hear God.

What "*YOU*" think stinks—listen to GOD!

When you spell a swear word, it's just like saying it.

Some will pout, but YOU obey without a doubt.

God's Word will keep you, as long as you keep it.

You can make your own words your worst enemy—by speaking negativity.

In all you do—do all you can do.

Evil people look for loopholes when they sin.

Always fight ignorance with intelligence.

Hardship will sift out so-called friendships.

The person who listens the most, will learn the most.

The mind of God is an understanding passed problems.

If you hear God—share God.

The shame of sin is the fame of sin.

No matter what you need, you will **<u>NEVER</u>** need greed.

You cannot find yourself by yourself, you need God.

Life won't make you happy, you have to make your life happy.

Let your flowers show God's power.

Food is good—don't worship it.

Your scheme is the devil's dream.

Don't let greed, hurt your seed.

If you want to win favor, win at obedience.

Learn to think before you sink.

Check your lawn for weeds and remove them devils.

In this life, what you get, is what you leave behind.

Success starts in Christ.

If you want the best from God, be your best for God.

When God speaks, there's nothing left to hear.

Trouble and problems are friends—they double team you.

Your success starts with God.

When you dress in faith—don't undress.

If you want to be elevated—elevate God.

If you are really righteous—everything you do should show it.

There is no wealth greater than good health.

When you pick up your Bible—your Bible picks you up.

Faith is your will working right.

If you eat wrong you won't live long.

Faith is like gasoline—it starts the car, but it's up to you to drive it.

If you have a bald head—God knows every hair you use to have.

Don't let your past pollute your future.

You live on earth, but keep your mind on heaven.

When you get upset, you get offset—upset offsets you.

The earth is a sea of sin—don't drown.

How can you have faith without faithfulness?

The devil will make you who you are NOT; God will make you who you ARE.

To disagree against sin is self-defense.

If you count on people you will become tired of counting.

If you do right by God, you'll get right from God.

If you want a life worth living—live a life of giving.

Bad correction is the wrong perception.

The devil knows your weakness—learn his weakness too.

The class of your friends can be the class of your sins.

Faith in man is faith in quicksand.

If you want people to love you—start loving people.

The wrong minded is wrong for your mind.

Heaven is within reach, if you would just reach for heaven.

When you've been through hell—you can deal with jail.

God knows what you need and you need what God knows.

People are like flying ducks—they find on leader and they follow.

The road to victory travels through humility.

Let your vision be your victory.

It's not real if it's not God's will.

It's not true if it's not God's rule.

It's not right if it's not God's light.

Christians own everything, because God owns everything.

The body doesn't think—it just wants.

People with faith are not suppose to say, "I'm trying to go to heaven." They're suppose to say, "I'm going to heaven!"

People who think they know it all is not as attentive as people who don't.

Let the light guide you right.

If you let God synchronize your heart with his you will stay on beat.

I'm God's son by adoption—my problems are God's by adoption.

Don't focus on what you did—focus on what you can do.

Without obedience there is no faith.

If God can get you to see where He stands then you can stand where He sees.

Help someone's need—not their greed.

If you're weak—patch the leak.

God knows that when you truly start hating sin—you truly start loving Him.

God knows that we're dirty—that's why He sent Jesus, so we don;t have to roll in the mud.

Sometimes a Christian will say "Who know?" Then he remembers—God knows.

A plant who keeps growing back to a seed can never grow into a tree.

When you fail God—you fail.

God enjoys life—that's why He created life.

Start speaking what God says speak.

Street life is the doorway to prison life.

Don't just carry the Word—let the Word carry you.

When you hate sin—you won't treat it as a friend.

Christians will never die spiritually—only physically.

Heavenly faith agrees with God, earthly faith does not.

You are in this world to do something for God.

Christians who go through a lot, remember—Christ is worth a lot.

Real Christians don't fight with their hands—they fight on their knees.

It's impossible to stay saved and not fear God.

In Christ, to grow up, you must step down.

When you don't have control of your mind, you don't have control of your life.

Everyone who says, "Crime pays," are saying, "Sin pays," they're liars.

If the devil can deceive you, he can defeat you.

Obey the gospel—**not** the law, because the gospel fulfills the law.

The devil will plant mines in your mind to think on — to explode.

Faith is the wire that connects you to God's power.

What is normal to God, is supernatural to man.

If you are saved, the power of what God speaks is waiting for you to speak.

Righteousness is a gift—holiness is up to you.

God thinks of everything at the same time—can you?

Deceit follows defeat.

God's mind is knowing everyone's mind at the same time.

If you're still perverted, you're not converted.

When you're set free from the enemy—you don't act like the enemy.

The more you change things—the more things change.

You cannot sleep with the wicked and wake up with the righteous too.

If you sleep with the devil you will become pregnant with sin.

The road to success is measured by faith.

If you don't fear the Lord—you're not saved.

Whoever you don't like—love them until you like them.

Love mends every flaw and removes every wall.

When you put your trust in man—you put your trust in trouble.

If you're still acting like the enemy—you're not free.

The more you are polite—the more things become light.

Prison life is still life.

Positive thoughts strengthen the mind—negative thoughts weaken the mind.

Some Christians seek God's hand and not His heart.

Life is strange when you make God a stranger.

Every penny you give is a penny you earn.

Christians don't need to defend God—we need God to defend us.

The wicked eats sin like a rat eats cheese.

A positive mind cannot be comfortable around negative thinkers.

Only a hypocrite would think he is inside of Christ, operating outside of Christ.

Shoes won't shine—if you don't shine them.

A godly mind is light, an ungodly mind is darkness.

Sinners don't win and winners don't sin.

A godly man has his lights on and God is home.

When you were born death was there and he will never forget you.

A changed mind shows a sign of change.

For every penny you spend, there's a penny you will have to make again.

In the Bible God never curse—why do Christians curse?

Fighting is only an answer to the ignorant.

Cursing is the way that satan speaks; God's Words are Holy and Pure.

Swearing is not fearing God.

Swearing never existed until sin existed—words that God can't stand to hear.

Satan even speaks to the deaf people, he knows their minds can hear.

In this world there are true Christians and false Christians.

Man's mind thinks of one thing at a time, but God's mind thinks of everything at the same time.

Just because Christians are friendly to the wicked—doesn't mean they are friends.

There is a difference between friendly and friendship. To be friendly is to be kind, to have a friendship involves a relationship and trust.

Faith never says "No," it says, "Let's go!"

When you live recklessly sooner or later you're gonna wreck.

If you want to be blessed continue to do God's will.

Caring is not swearing.

The righteous knows a lot of things that the wicked doesn't know they know.

When sinners say "You've changed," they mean it for the bad, but God changed you for the good.

No matter how people treat you, you still have to answer to God for how you treat them.

God rebukes negative minds. Strong Christians should rebuke negative minds too-not only in word, but in deed.

It is impossible for the righteous to be friends with the wicked—to honestly be friends would mean God approves of it.

For a Christian to have friendship with the wicked is like light having friendship with darkness.

The only way Christians could have a true friendship is on the same accord with God.

Walk in the light of love, which shows the love of the Light.

Don't let your mouth be your weakness.

A lie blinds—the truth reveals.

A lie binds—the truth frees.

Anything that is used less become useless.

Don't ever let someone's altitude change your answer.

Don't ever let someone's attitude change your altitude.

If you love your family, get saved, so God can save them too.

A person who really loves God, will look for things to do that God loves to do.

Only God can clean up what you messed up.

Men who don't control their tongue, think it means they're strong minded. It actually means their weak minded—the world can't control their tongues.

If you're riding in a limousine with God—why get on the bus with the devil.

If you're dumb enough to fall, be smart enough to call JESUS.

Every time FAITH shows up, fear leaves .

The faster the tongue—the more slippery the way.

People who put faith in earthly things—are as dumb as a dog chasing it's tail.

Don't rehearse the curse, rehearse the blessings.

Don't give up—live up!

Forgiving is living!

Do not conceal love—reveal love.

Let you life glorify God's glory!

The best teacher follows the Creator.

If you want to live—live to forgive.

Jealousy hates giving credit.

You cannot obey the devil and see God.

The is failure in fear, but favor in faith.

Love never has to talk—love is action.

Whoever the devil hinders—God can render.

When faith is born, fear dies.

Without God, we are as blind as bats flying in darkness.

If you don;t think of your future, you will keep thinking of your past.

When God lights your candle, don't blow it out.

If the earth exists then Heaven exists. The Word that created earth also created Heaven.

Some people think you're strange because you act different, but what's strange is people who look different and act the same.

There is no selfishness in righteousness.

Negative thinkers put more energy into what they find wrong, instead of what they can find right.

A negative mind thinks negative about positive things.

Love **NEVER** gives up, that's why JESUS didn't quit.

Your actions are a manifestation of your thoughts.

Let your life glow in God's glory.

Even when you walked in sin God had miracles waiting—for you to become His friend.

Good behaviors bring favor.

Every time you lie, satan lied to you.

The devil lies to you, then you lie to God.

Wisdom is obeying God's wisdom.

If a person is disobedient, don't let them infect your obedience with their opinions.

Faith never fails us—we fail.

Wisdom is how you use God's knowledge.

FAITH is believing God—NOW!

To walk with God, you cannot work with satan.

Speak what God speaks to you.

If you don't do what Jesus is saying—you're paying.

Give God your life—to do with it as He pleases, not as you please.

You cannot tell a lie without satan telling you the lie you told.

Only the wise can improvise.

If you're acting like the devil, and God kicked the devil out of Heaven—why would you think God would want you?

Why do you think God would allow a devil back in Heaven when He already kicked one out?

You do the possible and God will take care of the impossible.

The devil will trick you into getting high and then living his lie.

If you are acting like the devil you are going with the devil. If you are acting like Jesus, you are going with Jesus.

God and the devil are total opposites. If you disobey one you will obey the other.

Why worry about a few years on earth when eternity lasts forever?

The moment you focus on what you do have, you won't focus on what you don't have.

God will give you the wisdom to think past your own understanding.

Christians don't argue with the devil, so why do they argue with God?

Where there is no holiness, there is no righteousness. Keep doing positive things and something positive is more possible to happen.

Some people have to hit the bottom before they will reach up to God for help.

If you invest in your body, it will payoff in good health.

Let your walk speak louder than your talk.

Sinners and backsliders are married.

Remember, sin can come by hearing too.

When God loves you, it doesn't matter who doesn't like you.

Sinful songs sow sinful seeds.

God can use the devil, but the devil cannot use God.

The secret to life is waiting on Jesus.

Only the impossible is possible with God.

Whatever you have to face, it has to face God—if you're a Christian.

To Change you have to rearrange.

The devil wants you high, so you can live a lie.

Your obedience will help God to finish His plans for you.

Nobody minds helping you, when it benefits them.

God doesn't have opinions—just facts.

I love faith because it works with God.

If you are a believer—continue to believe.

People with no faith will help satan steal yours.

Are you fit or counterfeit?

If you keep thinking back, your mind will work backwards.

With God—if you stop, you flop.

You have never fathered a lie—the devil is the father of lies.

If you let just anyone into your life—they can bring anything into your life.

Is your life claiming of shaming the Christian walk?

God is willing to help you obey, but He will not force you to obey.

It is better to be a man of God than a god to man.

Greed says *"You need more, you need more."* If you're greedy—you'll obey.

Greed never stops saying *"You need more."*

Disobedience is like lying, because when you don't obey God, you're living a lie.

Holy Inspired Poems

In this section, the next ten pages are poems. These poems are written just as God gave them to me. I pray that you have been blessed by this book.

This is Volume II of III, keep a look out for Volume III of **'The Vision of Wisdom: Holy Inspired by God'** coming December 2016.

I'm Healed

God's presence from above—
descended as a dove

Shekinah Glory—manifesting His agape love
I'm steppin' and checking—exposing every lie
walking circumspectly with my spiritual eye

Peddle to the medal—faith chasing fear
got the devil on the run—ALL Heaven cheer!

Prayer warrior—praise on the battlefield
He took 39 stripes—that's why I'm healed

Helmet of Salvation and my two edged sword
crushing evil with The Word

Real deal—demons coming left and right
I'm praising God and speaking light

Knees to the ground, tears falling down—
fighting against the enemy, for my crown

Kingdom go God, deep in my heart
He's coming back—earth's getting dark

Don't Ask Me!

People ask, "Is there life on another planet?"
My answer is, "If so, God planned it."

They ask, "Do you believe in U.F.O.'s?"
"I don't know what's out there, only God knows.

The Bible we have is for this place—
God inspired it for the human race

"Are we the only one's who exist?"
"No, there's Heaven in the north,
past the stars we list.

Maybe the things we can't explain,
are too far past the abilities of our brain.

Most Powerful Friend

A bolt of lightning is a spark—compared to His
Sun which divides the day from dark

He separates the sea boundaries, to give us land
made a woman from a rib, out of the side of man
And placed all the stars with His wit—
just like a candle, each one God lit

So REPENT and make God your strong tower—
His name is Jehovah, the Most High Power

Divine design the whole Universe—
Synchronize the entire Cosmo course

Left His abode for the redemption of sin
God is calling you to become His friend

My Turn to Live

I thank God, I am the only me
that ever existed

I am the only me
that was ever invented

I am the only me
that GOD personally minted

I am the only me
Thank God I was created!

Alone in My Cell

Alone in my cell—is my living hell
God help me please—speak to Governor Rell
Deep in my thoughts—in pain and faults
Thinking of home, and feeling alone

Learning the rules—what's wrong and right
This is my story—this is my song
No one to call—no one to phone
Thinking of home, and the wrong that I've done

Hating my crime, and missing all of the fun
Tears in my eyes from all of the lies—
the people I hurt, their pain and their cries
Please help me God, looking out at the sod

Four walls to fight and no freedom in sight
I just want to yell—"Let me out of this cell!"
I will calm down, if you bring me my mail

My name in the paper and my name on the news
Can you understand why I'm crying the blues?
Just watch the road that you chose
If you're smart, you won't make my moves

Earth Spin Faster

As the earth spins fast—my troubles will pass
As man keeps time—I will pay for my crime
As the day turns dark,
on my calendar another mark

As I lay in my cell—thanking God it's not hell
As I pray to God for help, pleading this pain I felt
—with tears dripping on my pillow, knowing I can
sleep, when the noise gets mellow

The freedom to sleep, is the freedom to share
and the freedom to breathe, the God given air
As I look out my window, never felt so low
It could be worse, I'm not on death row

As I finish this letter and come to the end
thanking the Lord for being a friend
I was washed in the blood of His Son
"Carry my cross—if you think it's fun."

Hallelujah

Glory Hallelujah, I sing
Heaven and earth, knows Your name
You are the lover of my soul,
Into the Holies—I come bold
with prayer, supplications and request,
knowing forever—I AM blessed

God created my new heart
Thank You Lord for a brand new start
You accept me as Your son
the devil is defeated—CHRIST has won

From the Heaven to the earth
into Mary she gave birth
The Angels witness a Miracle
a baby's born—supernatural

Came to save us
from ALL sin
He is Christ—but God within

I'm Saved Now

Angels watching over me
guard my feet—what I don't see.

Hallelujah to the King
Heaven and earth together sing.

Come to visit from above,
bringing gifts of Holy love.
Shower with your latter rain,
on my knees I cry your name.

Enter deep inside my heart,
seek Your wisdom from the start.

Falling Angels after me,
in the North, I call on Thee.
No one takes me from Your hand—
lead me to the promised land.

On My Way Home

Walking worthy, not in shame—
on my forehead is Your name.

Was in darkness, now in light—
Holy highway is in sight.

I spread Good News throughout the land,
loving kindness of Thy hand.

On my way, be there soon,
in the north, pass the moon.

On the road to Your home,
in the Spirit, not alone.

Angels singing songs to Thee
I see Your gates in front of me.

Tears

Not one tear was wasted here,
bottled up—He'll show you there

Pain and sorrow, left on earth
pray to God, He knows your worth

Red eyes, all left behind,
you'll witness not one evil sign.

Never night, always day
He is The Light, He is The Way.

The Vision of Wisdom Artwork by Gerald Filyaw

All Sorts of Sports

Construction Site

to view/purchase more artwork go to:
http://gerald-filyaw.pixels.com

Miracle of the Loaves and Fish Shop ®
Expect a miracle - - everyday!
Matthew 14:13-21

Here are a few of the Miracle of the Loaves and Fish products. To view jewelry, home goods and more products with the Miracle of the Loaves and Fish logo go to: http://www.cafepress.com/miracleofloavesnfish

Acknowledgements

I give all of the credit and glory to God because He is the power who inspired this book. Thank you Lord for creating this awesome book.

Special Thanks To:

My wonderful gifts from God, Shane, Priscilla, Kandyce, Sonny, Kelly, Duane, Jermaine and LaShawn, I love you all. My children, who have been through hell and high waters with me. Their love and forgiving hearts have blessed my life. Please forgive me for not being a better Dad years ago, but now I AM HEALED!!!

My mom and dad with all their love and understanding by faith and God, the only creator. God bless them, Rev. William G. Filyaw and wife Evangelist Geraldine Filyaw, who God used to help shape me, support me and raise me. I am so glad they're both in God's abode, Heaven.

My loving kind brother, William Filyaw Jr., who never stopped writing me every month, for nine years of prison. Your letters made me feel and know that you love me. I thank God for your true heart.

About the Author

Gerald Filyaw was born in New Haven, CT. to Pastor William G. Filyaw and Evangelist Geraldine Filyaw. Gerald spent most of his childhood in church.

When he was not in church he could be found on the basketball court. When Gerald was 11 years old, he began inventing and still enjoys inventing today.

Gerald started drinking alcohol at the age of 19, married at 20 and by the age of 21, he found himself addicted to using cocaine for over the next 26 years of his life.

His ungodly behavior ended in prison. It was at that time of solitude in his life that he received an awaking from God.

In 2003 he asked God for wisdom and God did just that, he gave Gerald Godly wisdom, it was then that The Vision of Wisdom began to come about.

Over the next eleven years, as God poured into Gerald (and He still does till this day) whatever paper he could find, and even inside the blank cover of his bible he would use it to write down the wisdom he receives.

Gerald is a high school drop out, but that did not paralyze God in the least from being able to use him for His glory. God is able to use anyone who will obey Him, to manifest His glory through and Gerald is grateful that God chose him.

Gerald has been given many gifts, one of which is an artist. His artwork has been displayed in art shows, public buildings, public schools and newspaper articles. The word of his art continues to quickly spread, as he continues to submit his gifts unto God.

Gerald Filyaw is a born again believer, father, inventor and artist. He has eight wonderful children that he has been blessed with, whom he loves dearly.

Author Contact Information

Email all inquiries to:
gfilyaw@divinepurposepublishing.com
Subject: Attention Gerald Filyaw

Publisher's Contact Information
placed here at author's request

DiViNE PURPOSE PUBLISHING Co., LLC
'WRITING WITH A PURPOSE'
WWW.DIVINEPURPOSEPUBLISHING.COM

DiViNE PURPOSE PUBLISHING CO., LLC
A Christian Based Book Publishing Platform

Eccl. 3:11 (GW) It is beautiful how God has done everything at the right time.

WRITING WITH A PURPOSE

(205)336-2277
www.divinepurposepublishing.com
info@divinepurposepublishing.com

DiViNE PURPOSE PUBLISHING CO., LLC
A DOBBS FUSION COMPANY

EVERYDAY LOW PRICES
WWW.DIVINEPURPOSEPUBLISHING.COM

	Basic reg. $1099	Deluxe $1999	The Works $3849	Extreme $4999
	$899	$1699	$3299	$5599

www.ingramcontent.com/pod-product-compliance
Lightning Source LLC
Chambersburg PA
CBHW031517040426
42445CB00009B/279